T0300684

SONGS FOR SOLO VOICE

JAMES R. WHITLEY

© 2021 James R. Whitley

Design and cover photograph © 2021 Susan Gardner
Author's photograph by Hafiz Irshad

All rights reserved. No part of this book may be reproduced in
any form, by any means, electronic or mechanical, without
permission in writing from the author, except for brief quotations
for the purpose of reviews.

ISBN 978-1-952204-06-7

Printed in the United States of America

RED MOUNTAIN PRESS

Seattle, Washington
www.redmountainpress.us

For Peggy Jean Matystik
who taught me everything I ever needed to know about faith

CONTENTS

I

How to Talk Your Way Through Abandonment

Say *affection, affliction, addiction.*

Then say *unrequited,* say it clearly.

Say *several random acts of unkindness were perpetrated.*
Say *evidently, just a naïveté wrapped in the thinnest skin.*

Say *an ensuing grief weighty enough to bring a body down.*

Say *countless quarts of rum raisin to dull the sting.*

(Sprinkle liberally with the appropriate modifiers,
like *brutally* or *dour-colored.*)

Say *she was not without her imperfections and yet...*

Say *at his most compromised, he would treat me with derision,*
without regard for my fragile nature.

(Don't say *wretchedness is the fated fuel of the crestfallen.*)

Say *hands clasped, desperately,*
in prayer,
in hopes of...

Then say *render unto Caesar that which is Caesar's.*

Say *endurable,* say *survivable.*
Say *I still believe despite...*

(Don't say *regret shall ever taint the days of the hopeful.*)

Say *soft rains and the smell of the ground.*
Say *a formal feeling comes.*

       (Don't say *regret.*)

Say *a species of grace hovering there,*
                  and always available for the taking.

Say *everything in its proper place then.*
Say *the party will surely have ended*
       if we don't shake a tail feather already.

Say *endurable.*
Say *survivable.*

Repeat as necessary.

OVERTURE

Listen closely, starving students,
as this choir of unforgiving cynics scolds
that he should have heard—

even before
the demanding contralto entered,
even at the oh-so-glorious beginning—

the melody already starting to break down,
the bleak chords and dour notes
disintegrating into a telling cacophony.

And the troubling story thus being told—
something about lack of harmony,
something about inevitable decay.

All of the early discordances,
forgivable, but still audible to
the observant listener,

still a threat to the larger opus
if it were intended to be
unblemished, undiminished.

A presaging of strident missteps speaking
less of control in the face of chaos
and more of an unstoppable slippage

into some other cycle, a heralding
of the tragic denouement sure to come
despite all the sincere effort put in.

HALVED, THEN QUARTERED

Then left for dead.

Then forgotten—
indiscretion's dusty carcass disintegrating in the attic corner,
the last few sour notes of a botched scherzo echoing off.

Tell me,
isn't that how a perfect crime unfolds?
How the felon maintains his shameless pattern of
breathing and eating and laughing and sleeping
without interruption?

       I am content to be standing here without you.

From the time-scarred vantage point of the overlooking cliffs,
one can see truth plainly:
that waves don't *break against*,
but *are broken by* the shore.

       I am content to be standing.

Although unacknowledged, unmet,
there is a need in this tainted world
for more eyewitnesses
or, at least, softer sand.

Piazza San Marco, 1996

Given the appropriate container,
a whole lifetime can be preserved—

an ancient beetle encased
in a solemn glob of amber,
a Cro-Magnon hunter trapped under ice.

And here:
a misplaced photograph I've yet to destroy.

In it, we're feeding pigeons in Italy—
your dark hair windswept, your dark eyes shut,
a perfect halo of Venetian sunlight
framing your face,

your arms fully extended,
palms upturned in invitation,
and me, kneeling beside you,
gazing up,

the chaos of so many eager wings,
the two of us caught up
in the flurry of all that hunger.

RETROSPECTIVE

Perhaps our voyeuristic gods expect too much of us,
inherently flawed creations that we are,
weak putty in the hands of temptation.

Despite the various edicts we've been issued
not to look back,
who among us could ever resist?

Think of the case of Psyche
ordered to tolerate the smooth hand groping her
from behind the veil of nightfall,

her curiosity burning
like melted candle wax
on her husband's immortal skin.

Or tragedy's poster boy
Orpheus and his impatient lyre—
something tapping him on the shoulder

as he climbed into sunlight just
steps ahead of his beloved Eurydice,
something hissing repeatedly in his ear,

Turn around
and check her out, man.
You know you want to.

And are we really expected to ignore
the knowledge incessantly buzzing
inside our inferior human heads?

Such an unreasonable demand since
even we lowly creations know that
in this ever-expanding universe of miracles

there is always something more to see and,
no matter the penalty, there is always
some compelling reason to look back.

A moment of silence now for Lot's wicked wife,
perhaps suddenly realizing that she'd left
the family poodle chained in the garage or

just wanting to catch that once-in-a-lifetime glimpse
of what an Armageddon looks like,
whatever her motivation,

turning to behold the something still back there,
the something singing her name from behind a flaming door,
rationalizing to herself,

Surely He won't begrudge me
one parting glance
considering all that I'm leaving behind.

THROUGH THE GLOAMING

Overhead, the blasé moon hangs
like a luminous wrecking ball,
a thirsty razor-sharp pendulum.

Stars glare down rudely like
cold unblinking eyes—
inquisitive, intrusive.

In my emptied home,
radiant with ruin,
I sit still, the way a fox,

hiding deep in thorny underbrush,
badly wounded,
sits:

though confused,
understanding enough
of the hunter's haste,

enough of the hound's
agitated growling
and barking

to know that this
desperate throbbing
could mean the end.

SOUVENIR

If I take it all back—
the jagged insults hurled like careless daggers,
the failing stargazer lilies and their accusations of neglect,
every unconscionably late anniversary gift—
could there be room left for negotiation?

Or, if not, an available room somewhere
with walls painted the color of possible pardon?

Despite the extrapolated significance of
my past misadventures, I'd like to believe
I am not among the lowliest of God's creatures

and that I'm not the intended subject
of this newspaper headline that reads:
"Twice-Bitten Fool Risks All On Obvious Long Shot,
Loses Big Time."

From this safer distance,
I can admit that I miss your heavy smoke,
your strategically-positioned mirrors,

the way you could whip up the heartiest breakfast
using just maple syrup and your body,

how you could stand in a simple slant of moonlight
and cast a shadow that looked remarkably like
that of a small animal struggling vainly in a vise.

And I'm thinking now of
Barbara Stanwyck's premeditating husband
at the end of *Sorry, Wrong Number*
begging his wife to leave the doomed house,
desperately trying to undo her imminent undoing.

And how, eventually,
there comes a point—
call it *reluctant acquiescence to*
or *three-toed epiphany*—

a point in that loaded space between
the song's ending
and when it's actually over,

a point when you realize
there's no salvaging miracle coming
and you know you have to hang it up
and let go already

or stand there,
numb, just listening
as the train rushes steadily toward
its next destination without you.

Thirteen Ways to Deny an Ending

1. Position your body between the door and his body, then turn to stone.

2. Spread your tears like thin ice beneath her feet, and then turn to glass.

3. Lecture like a doomsday astronomer—warn against the Earth without the sun, the tides without the moon…

4. Counter with a mathematical argument, perhaps something about the number 2 and natural balance or the number 1 being *too* odd.

5. Make up an excuse to exit the theater before the final act— if a curtain falls and you are not there to see it, then…

6. Rub raw onion (or any handy irritant) in your eyes and renew your faith in chemistry.

7. Imagine that you are merely playing tennis and redefine terms like *match, break, love…*

8. Rewrite history, especially the darker periods, and try to sell the revision as best you can.

9. Spin a yarn about a more palatable future—borrow tropes from works of fantasy or mythology, if that helps.

10. Shut your eyes tightly as if the light in the room is suddenly too bright.

11. Open your eyes wide and pretend you suddenly cannot see—feel free to proclaim sudden deafness too, if that seems useful.

12. Even if you don't believe, pray.

13. In front of a mirror, attempt strategies 1 through 12 again until…

SOSTENUTO

No matter how striking the tune,
the sound after a song has been sung
is no sound at all,

is silence actually, its own type of music.
And just before that: the art,
the awesome revelation of it echoing

out into and through experience,
so wanting to hold onto its place here,
receding from the ear

in noticeably reluctant waves,
each ebbing note perfectly seasoned with
that elusive spice the lapidary calls fire.

And then it's over.
And one trembling begets another.
And there is no proper key for longing.

Still imprisoned in a cell of stage light,
the drained alto voices her confusion,
What can any of it matter—

bass clef, treble clef,
hemidemisemiquaver—
now that the show has ended?

QUITE TAKEN

More hardened than hopeful,
mother said it best:
"Cheaters cheat and liars lie."

So there we have it, true believers—
a clear path forward, a way out,
and a reason not to break.

> And yet the mind can't seem to make itself up,
> continues challenging its own demands:
> *Resist, obey, resist, obey…*

But does that justify laying down
this trail of sticky-sweet crumbs
to lure the fantasy back home?

Does it explain my pleas for mercy
that continue long after the church
has crumbled to dust around me?

> And the worn heart, with its warped gospel,
> still goads:
> *Dare, jump, dive…*

In time, the mask tears, salt burns the wound,
and the scab lifts, just enough,
to reveal the restive story beneath it.

And, finally, I hear a hymn playing and
I panic, I pray, I hail Mary.
You hail a cab.

HERE

We would like only, for once,
to get just where we are already.
-Martin Heidegger

Finally, a plausible theory:
that, hate it though I do,
this often stygian place—

call it *frosted-over afterglow* or
unholy event horizon from which
no hope escapes—

is not just *where I am,*
but *where I am meant to be.*

And the moon glowers down here.
And the wind wails in vain, all day.

So I'm sliding Guatemalan worry dolls
underneath each extra bed pillow and
hanging dream catchers from my bowed ceilings
to capture anything even remotely shaped
like salvation.

And although there is no beach or lake nearby,
I'm distilling some random bits of meaning
from my neighbor's unsolicited counsel:

Tired swimmer,
with your teary-eyed view of the shore,
don't give up.

Ah,
so this is what the world looks like
from the epicenter of grief—

all dulled sheen and doubt-stained,
all faithless.

II

STOP ME IF YOU THINK

You've heard this one before:
hopeful and horny boy meets sucrose and cinnamon girl,
and then someone whispers the words *surrender to me*
and somehow makes them sound harmless.

And then another hapless someone
gets caught in the throes of…

If nothing else, you've taught me
to appreciate a well-crafted plot twist and
that no story is written until it actually is.

Though admittedly odd, I've begun
adding salt and lemon to my morning coffee
so as not to lose my taste for you completely.

And I've grown to favor winter over the warmer seasons
for how its abundance of ice
seems to reduce the swelling of regret.

My charming devastation, my delicious chaos,
I'm forging something of a life from this stubborn desire
to continue on as more than a mere cautionary tale
of lacerated muscle and failed light.

And I'm returning to the dance floor
despite the unsteady beat,
despite the memory of our fickle shadows
spreading across that lush expanse of possibility,
shuddering.

CONTEMPLATIVE

In a package of minutes there is this We.
How beautiful.
-Gwendolyn Brooks

In a package of minutes
there is this We,
there is this constant gnawing,
from within my skull and rib cage,
to admit that You were here,
that I invited You in.

In an otherwise dark corridor,
there was that fading apparition
We naively named "Our Future"
hovering before Us,

and that pine box in the corner
that might have been a coffin or
just a trunk for storing sweaters.

Here, the slipknot that is the heart
doggedly thumps out its plea,
release, release,

as if to communicate that salvation
might be nothing more than a yank
of a looped string, a mere tug
on a yet-to-be-discovered lever.

How disturbing.
How ingenious.
How beautiful.

SOMETIMES A LIGHT

Hovers about as aura,
pierces as insistent beam,
or floods the scene
to begin its framing or reframing,
its giving of depth, context, perspective...

And to think it all starts with
a faint ping of luminescence insinuating itself
into an otherwise dim world.

And sometimes the soft rapping
of opportunity is heeded,
the grim specter of regret
anticipated if the brass ring
were to remain unseized.

            I think this means we are forgiven.

It's becoming clear to me now that
we must be little more than tiny motes
floating past the ever-watchful eyes of God,
a mere hiccup in a vast field of surplus data,
a stray lyric dissolving, like salt,
into the warm water of time.

            I think this means we're free
            or, at least, that I am.

AN EXPLICATION

Is that the vaunted moral then?
That, together,
we were the completed story?

We were deep into its mysterious unraveling,
maundering through and over
the jagged plot lines and plot twists.

> *Do you see now how a maze,*
> *if given the chance,*
> *can embed itself within another maze?*

And, even if we had it,
what could "direction" have meant
in such dizzying heat?

The hapless blades of grass
ablaze in our heaving shadows.
Everything caught up in the inferno of us.

> *Can you see how a labyrinth*
> *will insist on asymmetry?*

Consider for a moment
the colors assigned to loss—
the much-hyped grays and black,
the hackneyed shades of blue.

But why not that wicked purple,
those flirtatious yellows and greens?
All were in the field that summer.
All are guilty then.

Do you understand now
how a path lives its double life
as both entry and egress?

Somewhere, right now,
someone is breaking something
that can never be fixed.

And somewhere, surely,
you are lying
in the nude—

your sweet cinnamon skin glistening
in a dark red room.

And you are not alone.

I think misery is the length of
the knotted string of details
between my scorched hands and that room.

I think that's it then:
we were the story.

We are how it will be told.

RECOVERY GHAZAL

As sharks near, the herring school into an agitated silvery cloud.
If grief strikes, spread among a group, it must be easier to bear.

The emptied home has its concerns as well: now who will fill
the ice trays, the deserted bed? And who needs so much beer?

Daily, I find a fresh victim buried under every fable, like poor
Goldilocks who I think was framed by that shifty baby bear.

The crotchety miser in me wants to let nothing go—not these
moldy bagels, this spare penny, that dream, this coarse beard.

Finally, the lesson flits in, stays: given time, every riven soul
can heal, no matter if stitched through with loss or threadbare.

RAW

Emptied of everything except this
multi-chambered sense of failure,
the brittle shell of a house shivers.

The bare floors moan underfoot.
The windows chatter like teeth.
I am now sole owner of

these creaking doors,
this garish vacancy,
the waiting mouth of the fireplace.

Outside,
the banshee wind offers
an impromptu leitmotif.

A snowshoe hare bounds away
as an aged oak succumbs
under the intolerable gravity of ice.

Undeterred, winter,
like every other cold actor here,
will continue doing what is its nature:

laying burdens,
freezing,
breaking.

EXCURSION INTO PHILOSOPHY

It seems the opened book has led him
to question what he thought he knew as truth,
as if something between its covers
has presented itself as a viable alternative.

Note the unobstructed light, in well-mannered
rectangles on the floor and wall, behaving like
a mathematical proposition, a known quantity.

And note the weighty concern furrowing
the man's brow as he sees something in the light—
perhaps a brilliant nexus there bridging the space
between the known and the potentially knowable.

Still, he stays seated on the edge of the bed,
only daring a tentative half-step into that
something glittering before him like progress.

Perhaps if he could understand the sleeping woman
and the undeniable question mark of her body,
then maybe he would finally have answers.

And what if everything the man needs
is there in the room with him already?
What then could the open window mean—
agape mouth through which what?

And so we are left with the drama
raging in this seemingly still picture:

the soft knowledge of flesh
brushing against some other flesh,

the perspectives of confused men and
confusing women barely touching,

the imposition of light setting ablaze
the uneasy geometry of longing.

Sonoran Desert, 1998

Our self-appointed mission that year:
to choke adventure from
the parched throat of Arizona.

And what you would later describe
to our former friends simply as
a wonderful vacation,

I still recall, in nightmares, as
Nature's blistering invective
against human frailty.

All the desiccated while there,
you in your own remote space,
admiring life's cameos

on that sandy stage—
the gaudy blooming
creosote and cacti,

those chatoyant cicadas fanning
themselves like church ladies
in the shade of a Joshua tree,

that diamondback rattlesnake
and its many-jointed argument
for persistence,

and me, focusing on
likely outcomes, wondering
why anything would stay in

such an unforgiving climate,
pitying every sweaty creature there
obviously thirsting for something.

Aubade, With Recurring Jay

I
Despite the dour skies,
a hopeful jay sings dawn in.
Two clouds part. Two more.

II
I wake up humming.
You are dressing in silence,
in dark grays and blues.

III
The breeze carries in
so much: the sure smell of rain,
pollen, dander, doubt.

IV
Confused, the jay sees
my graceless pacing and then
forgets his bright tune.

V
Still, something lies with
me, troubles the air as my
garden weeds over.

VI
Silently it waits
in the willow's bare branches
like a songless jay.

VII
Regret leaves a scar
like a failed duet, like a
song for solo voice.

SOMEONE FELL: A CALENDELLE

Though flawed, wings are rarely a bad idea. Think of the aviary,
how the stately crows and crown pigeons seem to never worry
about the ravenous raccoons skulking nearby—safety, just an arch
of a back, an urgent splay of feathers away. At my lonely table,
a man is sulking, ignoring the artifice of this bistro's name: *Chez
Plaisir*. Bathed in waning candle-glow, his face is a scarred moon,
anguish pooling in two of its craters, angst clouding over the sky.
Perhaps regret is the burnt chicken he just ate or the nonplussed
moth stuck in orbit around the dim streetlamp. Still, I remember
soaring like Icarus, an overeager sparrow chirping *how I got over*
even as the naïve wax began to melt, even as fate, once so tender,
revealed itself to be an abyss none can fly over, a sad spent ember.

EXCERPTS FROM A SURVIVOR'S JOURNAL

August 20th

And I thought it was strange that it would start raining,
so deep into the summer as it was and such a scorcher.
But the sunshower was a blessing—no one complaining
about the wet t-shirts, no one upset that the torture
had been stopped, at least momentarily. And while I
reveled in the cooling reprieve, you e-mailed that foul
cowardly message, ending an era. Despite the heat, my
entire body began to shiver as I thought about how
the savvy Luddites warned of technology's destructive
tendencies and how it would be our ultimate undoing.
More rain fell. Nothing left to do, I reasoned, but live
like a hopeful jay with a red wound on its blue wing.

September 18th

Like a hopeful jay with a red wound on its blue
wing could make me so late for work. Yeah right.
Still, when the crippled creature limping on its two
determined legs appeared at my door, the grim sight
of it stopped me cold. But it must have been nine
o'clock already, so I can't blame the fading bird
struggling to escape my neighbor's sadistic feline.
The mangled jay chirped what I swear was the word
"pity" as its essence oozed from its punctured wing
like so much wasted sherry. Across the yard, the cat
glared at me while licking its eager claws. Noticing
the time, I shut my door and stepped over the mat.

October 9th

The time I shut my door and stepped over the mat,
then fell—hard, ego-first—down the icy front steps,
you laughed your rude ass off. To be fair, perhaps
you didn't see snow blushing under me or hear the crack
of my surprisingly brittle arm against the indifferent
pavement. But still, laughter? I'll always remember
that howl more chilling than any New England winter,
even more painful than the break. Message sent
and received. Now, as autumn leaves cycle through
their moody reds and yellows—*it's dying time
again*—I'm thinking of what falling teaches us. I'm
thinking about the things I don't miss about you.

December 9th

Thinking about the things I don't miss about you—
the onion-skinned alibis, your crass flossing in bed—
I sift through some of the shinier thoughts instead:
our sex marathons lasting from midnight until noon,
lying bare-assed on the patio after, gorging ourselves
on your infamous pumpkin cheesecake and mojito.
Just folly in the wind now. *L'amour est un oiseau
rebelle.* I still have your silk thongs and bookshelves,
the cd's you said you loved but left, this scar just under
my ribs. Funny, huh? Finally told my nosy therapist
your name. *Think of your glass as half-full,* she insisted,
imagine your life regaining its luster, its thunder.

January 20th

Ed, imagine your life regaining its luster, its thunder as
you frolic through every hotspot in Milan and Paris,
the unctuous travel agent urged. But I had to pass
on the idea since he couldn't even get my name right
and, more than any Euro-jaunt, I was starting to miss
the soft rays of summer days, pearl-blue moonlight
mild enough that we...I mean, "I" could sprawl out
naked on the patio after dark. Alone at my bedroom
window, I watched the brazen pigeons openly flout-
ing a blizzard's fury, the gruff wind bullying long-
dead leaves. I decided then to escape the gloom
by heeding the Caribbean's lush call, its balmy song.

February 14th

By heeding the Caribbean's lush call, its balmy song
tempting like a Siren's mythical hex echoing, "Come
to me, spent sailor," I was renewed and, before long,
my devastated muscle thawed out after simmering
daily in the water glistening there like liquid topaz.
I squeezed in a tour of the St. Thomas ruins also: ling-
ering patina of majesty on the sun-dappled flutings,
the tamarind-heavy breeze whispering "relent" as
it eased through the aged slats of louvered openings,
every jagged edge smoothed by time's rough hand
as if to prove that the stalwart can maintain some
grace, even in the face of adversity, and still stand.

February 28th

Grace, even in the face of adversity and still standing
after guzzling down four guavaberry daiquiris, somehow
kept her composure as we sighed goodbye at the airport
in Puerto Rico. Or maybe her name was Caryn. Or maybe
it was Jose. Whatever. My sojourn on those coddling
islands was full of such unnameable joys—every crowd-
ed beach and empty bar stool another gleaming proxy for
a possible cure. On my reluctant return flight to Bean-
town, the propellers' growl replaced the fragile pleading
of coqui frogs—yet another example of erosion, of how,
as Achebe warned, *things fall apart*, despite all efforts
to stop the song's trembling notes from fading eventually.

April 11th

To stop the song's trembling, notes from fading, eventually
I let it all go. To fuel forward movement, I've gone back to
snacking on soy nuts and self-pity. Now, in my bedroom
mirror, I'm lip-reading intently as my know-it-all reflection
scolds, "Poor Pagliaccio with your painted moue: you put
it on, you can always take it off." So, along with my thinning
hair, I'm brushing away regret. And, like my life generally,
my lingering pang of guilt has very little to do with you.
Last fall, I left a desperate blue jay to face the certain doom
of feline bloodlust. Brut-drenched, I must've smelled, to him,
like rescue. My dear diary: faith is not the firm surface my foot
and I thought it was. Strange that it would start raining.

HERE, FINALLY

A plausible theory is one that
points to a possible end to a quandary,
one that sticks to the ribs like
homemade meatloaf and real mashed potatoes.

For the past several months,
some loser down the street has been
butchering the lush Strayhorn classic,
caterwauling almost every night.

Or maybe it was just the glum baritone
scatting nonsense in my head.

Or the sound of merciful rodents
chewing through the dog-eared stack of
unsent love letters in my closet.

And speaking more objectively now,
there comes a point when you realize that,
no matter how long or torturous,
no road is your enemy.

> And the moon does not *glower down*.
> And the wind does not *wail*.

On my outdated, but trustworthy, television set,
the game show contestant voices his selection to the host,
I'll take "Songs That Gravely-Wounded Animals Sing"
for a thousand, Alex.

Finally, I thought,
a category I know something about.

III

TREMBLING DELICIOUSLY

after Charpentier

But for the approaching storm,
the small boat would loll calmly
upon the water's blank surface,
would most assuredly be at ease.

And commenting further
on my long-held expectations
of the real world—
how everything may seem all
smiles, light and joy
one naïve moment, and then
Kismet gives you the finger—
despite the knowledge that
everything is skidding toward
a preordained entropy, we all
want to believe that,
once experienced,
bliss will linger somehow,
like the prodigal stars forever
able to share their brilliance.

My dear maudlin Louise,
take what you will from this—
still water, pale joy, some faith
even if riddled with suspicion—
but know that,
when it comes to loss,
none of us is immune.

An Epilogue

That the crocus bulbs arrived dead
and so long after the recommended
spring planting season that fated year,
you insisted,
was not the biggest tragedy,

rather
that only five were packed in the shipment,
when you had paid for a solid half dozen,
bothered you to no end.

So much of what we would, tactfully,
later refer to as
"the unmendable rift between us"
was evident even here:

me and my stubborn focus
on usefulness,

and you,
always counting the many luminous disasters
that added up to our life together.

I dredge all of this up to confess,
in my typically roundabout way,
that I'm not handling loss well—
the brutal turns and startling bumpiness of it,
the unintelligible semaphore of faith.

Before that first kiss, I could already
taste the many flavors of uncertainty—
overripe kiwi-melon lip balm,
wintergreen mouthwash masking
mentholated cigarette breath.

And still I dove—
discretion-first, knowingly—
into that experience, into that heresy
covered with such perfect skin.

INSIDE THE STORY OF IT

(a found poem)

Curious how the notion of it,
like a glance or an especially tough
course you have to run, can
shift suddenly.

> *It is a dumb habit or a great honor, is the big money*
> *shot, is a brief history of endemic disease, is a kind of*
> *luck or an ability to, is vanity or is not, is behind you or*
> *is not, is a brilliant musical score, is a closed library*
> *with the book you need in it, is that one special book,*
> *is the pretty snow falling on the trail we walked,*
> *is the beautiful silence falling with it…*

And how, say, a game played—
however badly,
however distressing the ultimate defeat—
was an option to win something.

And what that can mean.
And what it can't.

> *…is an eleventh hour victory, is a paradox: a profanity*
> *and a great reverence for, is that last brownie, is a small*
> *taste of rich ice cream, is the question I asked you, is*
> *what happened just after you replied, is a smart girl with*
> *pride in her handbag, is her smart handbag, is the poor*
> *loser who fortunately discovered a million…*

And so,
pretending not to like the flagrant
habit my eyes had of staring,
she ordered a coffee and,
casually,
asked my name.

A conversation ensued.

> *...is Christ simply smiling at you, is a helluva sandwich*
> *or is the something crucial in the middle of the sandwich,*
> *is the senior poet shrewdly working with structure, is her*
> *beautiful handwriting, is Bach and the Beatles, is part*
> *kind cleric and part loathed lawyer, is a waning music,*
> *is a waning...*

And yes,
I know you want me to explain why,
to pause and then come back to your question
with something better.

But I think there is a limit to
what we can know about it
and what we need to.

Or maybe there isn't.

THE FARMER AND THE SNAKE

after Aesop

As the teacher told the tale, the snake—
antediluvian symbol of deception and evil—
was found outside in winter, frozen stiff,
by the farmer—symbol of goodness and humanity.

The farmer, a kind but naïve soul,
pulled the hapless snake to his chest—
home of the beating heart,
supposed wellspring of man's benevolence—

and then, so the story went, carried the snake's
tubular body—dying and different and, by implication,
ostensibly undeserving—back to the farm and family,
the man's rustic castle with its expectedly loyal subjects.

The characters and settings thus forcibly arranged,
the story proceeds according to plan—
the cared-for snake warming then waking by the fireplace,
thanklessly attacking the selfless family.

Then the farmer, always the fearless savior and protector,
rushes in brandishing his trustworthy ax—
phallic symbol of the man's strength and power—
and hacks the snake into scaly villainous bits.

The story warns us that some creatures can't be trusted,
certain groups of them unworthy of our generosity.
But what the story lacks is balance, a proper means
of weighing the elements of significance,

like an absent, but necessary, fulcrum that supports
the respect for the individual, that appreciates
the nature of that particular snake and farmer,
the uniqueness of that farm and welcoming family.

What's missing is reality: not every farmer
is so kind, not every snake so ungrateful,
and some families and homes are themselves
unbearably cold.

Perhaps opening your heart and home are inherently
dangerous offers, necessarily involving risk.
But no challenge is ever properly hurled
at such a well-tailored answer.

And that, my friend, is why it's called a fable.

RECURRING NIGHTMARE

I hope that I never forget it:
those two figures in the distance
silhouetted by dusk,
shaking, despite the midsummer heat,

huddling together, struggling over
a piece of string between them,
trying, in earnest, to undo
the many knots in the length of it,

striving, together,
to solve the multiple riddles
complicating the thin link they share
before night falls.

And in the background:
some music playing like a siren or
the sound a hungry hyena might make.
And still that frantic pair,

rarely looking at each other,
barely talking, their desperation mounting
as the sun between and all around them
dwindles with the dying breeze.

And that receding light
almost mocking them
in its celebratory departure of
gold and orange and indigo and red.

That tired couple,
their failing industry,
those cruel knots, that darkness
closing in like destiny…

I hope that I never forget it.

ANOTHER RAVEN-HAIRED IMBROGLIO

If not "The Ultimate Avatar of Dejection,"
then I am nameless,
a mere scumbled image
of a ghost in a cracked mirror.

My bitter little cabbage head,
my avulsed wing,
I am surviving you.

And if the threatened rains fall,
I will welcome the downpour.

Throughout the unnerving trial,
I will embrace the process of
soaking and shaking as ablution
and endure.

REFLECTION OF LITTLE TO NO CONSEQUENCE

As I recall that night,
you told me you had something to sell—
something salty and salacious,
something 500 proof and almost certainly illegal,
something with dimples and at least six oily fingers,
something that smelled like burnt honeysuckle and treason,
something with a pied-à-terre just outside of Paris.

Together, we stared into that feral sky as
thunder played its earnest jazz in the background.

The clouds were shaped like broken honey jars.

I spewed moscato across the room
every time you told a joke.

You complimented my cologne repeatedly,
even though I wasn't wearing any.

We made up pet names for each other.
I believe you called me "Lust-filled Louie"
or was it "Ne'er-Do-Well"?

I know I called you "Pyrite" and I meant it.

At the end of our last night together,
you laughed in my face and,
because I got the joke,
as I remember it,
I laughed along with you.

SHE HANGS BRIGHTLY

for Janelle

First, she turns into shadow,
then myth—
her body a falling half note

as it strains toward the door
then fades into yesterdays,
the moon a lost silver ball

hovering pointlessly
throughout that lengthy
first night without her.

And through the open windows:
the perfume of dying freesia
wafting in,

its sweet threnody—
though slight, diminished—
still cleaving the air.

You sit, still, on that bed
where you caressed her hands
and intercepted faithless pillows

slipping from her weakening grip
countless times.
Trust me when I say

you will survive this,
despite the difficult music
lurking in the background.

This is just the music
of never-forgetting-her,
the score of the rest of your life.

GINGERLY

Should there remain a day
beyond this attenuated night,
which, to me, seems like
some dark final statement,
I think I would like to see it and
begin, again, collecting memories
of the large bright door
swinging open suddenly,
of budding asters—
all gala and promise—
gathered for spontaneous presentation.

Despite the several meanderings
this faulty compass may
have me endure, I believe
I would like to walk the worn path again,
next time, perhaps, taking more
chary steps under the moon's
watchful pale blue eye.

So now, to this end, I pray nightly
to the beneficent god of
healing-completely-after-perfidy,
lay all my meager hopes
on the sweet angel of
letting-go-and-moving-on-already.

RESTORATIVE

Recall those first fertile moments—
some future, ripe with possibility,
blazing in her eyes,
something more than a hush
enthralling the restless city, and,
because it was sincerely-wrought, artless,
trembling lips and fingers touching
trembling lips and fingers.

Oh, worn palimpsest,
brash stricken idolater,
let it go.

Now, embrace this sweet invitation—
the undeniable music teasing the air
like a glorious overture to some
grand opera stirring up again,
the weighty curtain of acceptance
moving aside, finally,
to let the impatiently waiting light
rush in again.

Here, Finally, a Plausible Theory

In the unblocked spillway of the heart,
there is always an epic in the making.

      Beyond the tightest lips,
        there is a story dissolving under the tongue.

Even if secretly, everyone yearns
for a day of wine and roses,
a balmy night or two in Tunisia.

      If you parry and lunge,
        then I will repulse and thrust.

A game that yields no winner
is no longer a game.

      Regret is a threat lurking in the reliquary,
        an imperfect stitch in the heart's selvage.

Though sometimes hard and cold,
the world is more than just slate, schist and shale.

      Dusk is truly the time for lovers
        for see how they venture forth now,
        see how the sky coaxes them out
        all robed in claret, crimson, oxblood, vermilion.

IV

CODA

Again, the soothing refrain
looping its way back in.
Again, the infectious hook,
a kind of beacon beckoning,

Return to me.

And to think I only ever
wanted this: some shore
with no need for a warning
scribbled on its calm face,

the flotsam behind me
once again,
some generous reprise
called "peace-of-mind" and,

even if unaccompanied,
some relatively warm bed.
And to be able to say
We had quite a time that year

and not burden those words
with connotation,
not to imply
I pray we can live the dream again.

And, with some metronome slavishly
stitching the worn minutes together,
to get back
on the steady beat again.

And, even if unaccompanied,
to sing once more,
to make the expectant air tremble
deliciously with that rare something

most accurately described as
"hope-in-the-face-of,"
that muscular melody, like this morning
with no trace of yesterday staining it,

several octaves now above the blues,
leggiero.
And, finally, to hear
the dawn's rousing pronouncement:

Sweet aching child,
I have come with a new lyric.
In time,
you will learn it.

NOTES

"How to Talk Your Way Through Abandonment": This poem contains lines from Sara Teasdale's poem "There Will Come Soft Rains," Emily Dickinson's poem "After Great Pain," and the Bible, Luke 20:25.

"Here": The quote by German philosopher Martin Heidegger is from his work *Poetry, Language, Thought* (Harper, 1971) as translated into English by Albert Hofstadter.

"Contemplative": The quote by Gwendolyn Brooks is from the beginning of her poem "An Aspect of Love, Alive in the Ice and Fire" from her collection *Blacks* (Third World Press, 1987).

"Someone Fell: A Calendelle": A calendelle is a 12-line poem in which the final word of each line rhymes with a month of the year. This poem's antepenultimate line ends with the title of the gospel hymn composed by Clara Ward in 1951, which was later recorded by Mahalia Jackson, Aretha Franklin and others.

"Excerpts from a Survivor's Journal": "October 9th" contains the line "it's dying time again" which was inspired by the 1964 song "Crying Time" written by Buck Owens and made famous by Ray Charles. "December 9th" contains the opening line of the aria "Habanera" from Georges Bizet's opera *Carmen*. "February 28th" includes the title of Chinua Achebe's acclaimed debut novel *Things Fall Apart* (Heinemann Ltd., 1958). The "Poor Pagliaccio" appears in "April 11th" as a nod to composer Ruggero Leoncavallo.

"Inside the Story of It": This is a found poem composed entirely of words appearing in the first chapter of Erich Segal's bestseller *Love Story* (Harper, 1970).

"She Hangs Brightly": This title is inspired by the 1990 album and song of the same name recorded by the musical group Mazzy Star (Rough Trade Records, 1990).

"Here, Finally, a Plausible Theory": This poem references the song titles of "Days of Wine and Roses" by Johnny Mercer & Henry Mancini and "A Night in Tunisia" by Dizzie Gillespie.

ACKNOWLEDGMENTS

Grateful acknowledgment is made to the following journals in
which some of these poems were first published, sometimes
in different versions:

3rd Muse Poetry Journal (Australia): "Overture"
Aesthetica Magazine (United Kingdom): "Halved, Then
        Quartered"
Bare Root Review: "Souvenir" (as "Stop Me If You Think
        You've Heard This One Before")
Blood Lotus: "Excerpts from a Survivor's Journal"
Branches Quarterly: "Gingerly"
Can We Have Our Ball Back?: "Trembling Deliciously"
Facets: "The Farmer and the Snake"
FRiGG: "Contemplative," "Excursion into Philosophy,"
        "Restorative" (as "Apostasy")
Hidden Oak: "Through the Gloaming"
Identity Theory: "Recovery Ghazal" (as "What You Would Call a
        Loose Ghazal, I Regard as Another Small, but
        Necessary, Step Toward Recovery")
Pebble Lake Review: "How to Talk Your Way Through
        Abandonment," "Aubade, With Recurring Jay"
Poetry Salzburg Review (Austria): "Raw"
PW Review: "She Hangs Brightly" (as "Aria")
Strong Verse: "Retrospective" (as "What Lies Before You
        Might Not Be Your Future"), "Sonoran Desert, 1998"
Talking River: "Stop Me If You Think"
Texas Poetry Journal: "Someone Fell: A Calendelle"
The Dublin Quarterly (Ireland): "Sostenuto," "Here"
The Fictional Café: "Thirteen Ways to Deny an Ending," "Inside
        the Story of It," "Here, Finally, a Plausible Theory"
The Green Silk Journal: "Here, Finally," "Reflection of Little to No
        Consequence"
The Oklahoma Review: "Another Raven-Haired Imbroglio"
The Pinch: "Piazza San Marco, 1996"
The Strange Fruit: "An Epilogue"
Wilderness House Literary Review: "Sometimes a Light," "Coda"

An earlier version of "The Farmer and the Snake" appeared in the
chapbook *The Golden Web* (Wind River Press, 2003).

Thank you to Susan Gardner for being so generous with your time and insights, and for welcoming me into the Red Mountain Press family with such warmth.

Thank you to Lisa Rosenberg for selecting my manuscript and ending my 2020 on an unexpectedly high note.

Thank you to Gerville, Debbie, Myronical, Blim, Caryn, Adrian, Corrine and Julia Larsen for giving me more reasons to visit the Caribbean than just obscene amounts of sunshine and guavaberry drinks. *Mehsohn!*

Thank you to Fannie "Faneuil" Fong for decades of laughter and insanity in equal measure.

A solemn thank you to the memories of two poets who started my publishing career and blessed my boat, Naomi Long Madgett and Lucille Clifton—*dona eis requiem, sempiternam requiem.*

Thank you also to all of my supportive family members, friends and readers for sustenance that I rely on and am sincerely grateful for but could never begin to repay.

Songs for Solo Voice
is set in Garamond, a classic book font derived from the work of
the sixteenth century designer and publisher, Claude Garamond.